Baptismal Discipline

Colin O. Buchanan

Director of Studies at St. John's College, Nottingham
Member of the Church of England Liturgical Commission

SBN 901710 49 0

GROVE BOOKS

BRAMCOTE   NOTTS.

CONTENTS

First Edition March, 1972
Second Edition May, 1974

SBN 901710 49 0

PREFACE TO SECOND EDITION

The first edition of this booklet was published in March, 1972 and had completely sold out by Autumn 1973. There has been considerable evidence of its usefulness, sometimes (as in the parish of Clifton near to Nottingham) even leading to a thoroughgoing and gospel-centred parochial policy. I delayed reprinting it until General Synod could handle the subject in February 1974, and have consequently deleted the previous theological introduction, and replaced it with a brief account of Synod's treatment of the subject and the situation arising from that.

On the other hand I have hardly altered anything else in the booklet. The chapter on 'The Limits of Infant Baptism' could have been completely re-written to refer back, not to my essay in *Evangelical Essays on Church and Sacraments* (SPCK 1972), but instead to my fuller treatment of the subject in *A Case for Infant Baptism* (Grove Booklet on Ministry and Worship No. 20, 1973). However, in *Infant Baptism under Cross-examination* (No. 24, 1974) both writers have referred back to this one by page-numbers. It therefore was likely to be confusing to rewrite these pages. It would also have caused further delay, for a gain which would have been in arrangement, not in content. Anyone concerned about the whole principle of baptising infants should probably read nos. 3, 20 and 24 in succession.

Space might also have been found to review the book by R. R. Osborn mentioned on page 12, but I have done so elsewhere *(The Church of England Newspaper)*. Suffice to note that Osborn reckons that England to-day is still in Christendom. I do not. I cannot but see it as a genuine mission-field.

Colin Buchanan
30 April, 1974.

INTRODUCTION

In 1971 there were published two official Church of England reports relating to Christian Initiation:—*Christian Initiation: Birth and Growth in the Christian Society* by the Ely Commission, and *Baptism Thanksgiving and Blessing* by the Doctrine Commission.[1] These were briefly debated in General Synod in July 1971 and February 1972 respectively, but no decisions were taken, and they remained a responsibility of the Standing Committee of Synod. This body then asked the Rev. Peter Cornwell to take all the initiations question together and produce a 'Working Paper' for General Synod. This would enable the various issues to be set out objectively between one set of covers, and would lead to a clear set of practical proposals which could be put before the Synod. Thus, although the two original reports remained on the table, it would be the Cornwell Working Paper which would provide the material for the debate. And this Working Paper would of itself not so much propose solutions (as the earlier two reports had done) but rather isolate issues on which decisions would have to be taken.

The Cornwell document was completed in late 1973, and published as a Synod document (GS 184) in January 1974. It was introduced for a general debate in Synod by Peter Cornwell himself on 19 February, and then led to a series of practical resolutions, which were started on 22 February, but were not finished then and must come back at General Synod in July 1974.

However, the main issue which concerns this booklet—that of 'policy' (or 'discipline') in respect of infant baptism—was fully covered in the two debates, and was the subject of the first resolution passed in the second of them. It is therefore now possible to publish this second edition of this booklet against a fairly clear synodical background. The resolution passed by General Synod ran as follows:

> 'The General Synod adheres to the view that Infant Baptism should continue to be available to the children of all parents that request it and are willing *and able* to make the requisite promises, asks that the Liturgical Commission should note this expression of view, together with the requirements of Canon B21, B22 and B23, in the framing of any new Baptismal Services, *and commends, in particular, paragraphs 4 to 21 of the Working Paper for study in the Dioceses.'*[2]

It will be convenient to comment on each of the three main sentences in this resolution in turn.

1. '. . . all parents that request it and are willing and able . . .'

This resolution seemed calculated to prolong the days of 'indiscriminate

---

[1] Both were published by the Church Information Office, and both went out of print in 1973. They are being republished at the time of writing (May 1974) in a single volume.

[2] The two portions in italics were not part of the original platform motion moved by the Bishop of Ely, but were the result of two successful amendments from the floor of the Synod.

baptism' and even, through undermining the position of clergy and PCC's which already had a clear policy, to make the Church regress from any advances already made. I therefore tabled an amendment which read as follows:

> *'Leave out* all words after "General Synod" and *add:*
>
>> "notes the following paragraph in the Working Paper by the Rev. P. R. Cornwell:
>>
>>> 'The Church has to decide whether Infant Baptism should be administered to the children of parents who, not only make the promises, but also show evidence that they will fulfil them, or whether Infant Baptism should continue to be at the request of the parents, with the sole condition that they should make the promises. To decide for the former would involve a change in Church law. To decide for the latter would be to work within the framework of existing law'[1]
>>
>> and on this statement of the issue prefers the former view to the latter."'

This amendment was not intended to hold a gun at anybody's head, but merely to express a preference by Synod. However, after I had made my speech to argue the case, a member of Synod asked the chairman whether the amendment was not out of order on the ground that it was a bare negation of the platform motion. It was then ruled out of order on those grounds[2], and I had to find a new wording. I therefore changed the last two lines to read:

> 'and, recognising that both practices exist alongside each other in the Church of England, would welcome the opportunity to debate the desirability of the former view.'

It should be noted that the Cornwell statement of the issue may itself have been defective both in its emphasis on 'promises'—which is an inexact description of baptismal vows (see under 'new baptismal services' below)—and also in its statement of the present law (which was corrected by Christopher Wansey in the first debate and is also handled on page 12 below). However, it *was* the statement of the issue which lay before Synod. It should also be noted that my rewording would have produced an incredibly mild resolution, but it would have left one foot in the door.

In the event, two strong speeches supporting virtually indiscriminate baptism, had a powerful effect. Mrs. Statham said if she had not been allowed to bring her infant to baptism some years before, she would not

---

[1] This is paragraph 18, on page 9 of the Working Paper.
[2] There was an unfortunate note to this, because the Standing Committee had accepted the amendment when it had first been sent in, and the chair had apparently reached this opinion at the outset of the debate, and yet had still allowed me to make my speech before ruling the amendment out of order. This however is all water under the bridge now.

have been standing there in Synod as a believer at all. And Major Batt said a sermon of his the previous Sunday, when a party was present in Church at a baptism, had had a profound effect on one of the party, which it could not have done if the baby had not been admitted to baptism.[1] After all this, my amendment lost on a show of hands, gaining perhaps one-third of those present in its support.

One small change was made on an amendment when Christopher Wansey successfully moved the inclusion of the words 'and able'. This may have enabled some who had supported my amendment to vote for the amended resolution at the end of the debate. Although 'able' *might* mean no more than 'having the power of speech' (!), it was obviously intended to strengthen the resolution and turn it somewhat away from the 'indiscriminate' direction it was taking. On this interpretation the stance of the Synod may be declared slightly uncertain, perhaps ambiguous, but at least not very markedly worse than the position had been before.

2. '. . . . any new Baptismal Services . . .'

The Cornwell Working Paper suggested (paragraph 19) that the so-called 'promises' of Series 2 infant baptism were at variance with the law, and therefore should be altered if a policy within the existing law were determined. Paradoxically, Series 2 Infant Baptism was, in the same session of Synod, having its period of experimental use extended from 30 September 1974 to 31 December 1979. I therefore took occasion to point out, when provisional approval was being sought for this extension, that if the Synod accepted the argument that the Series 2 Infant Baptism 'promises' *are* inconsistent with the existing discipline, then it was no good voting for the former on the Thursday evening, and the latter on the Friday morning. Synod then did exactly that, and having underwritten the Series 2 'promises' has now asked the Liturgical Commission to bear the particular canons in mind (as though that would make any difference to the text).[2]

3. ' . . . and commends . . . paragraphs 4 to 21 . . . for study in the dioceses'

This was the part added at the end of the platform motion. It will be the responsibility of the Standing Committee of Synod to make available the requisite parts of the Cornwell Working Paper to the dioceses, but it is also true that the General Synod resolution will itself be before the dioceses for study and comment. As it is not clear that the diocesan synods will necessarily have resolutions to debate, it is important that those who go with the thrust of this booklet should ensure that the dioceses do not only 'study' the issue, but also express clear-cut findings on it. If, indeed, any diocesan synods (Chelmsford seems the most obvious example) should ask the General Synod to reconsider its own expression of opinion, then that would be considerable gain. Meanwhile, despite the somewhat fudged General Synod resolution, it should be clear that parishes, deaneries and dioceses are still free to make their own policy decisions in accord with the argument of this booklet.

---

[1] These are both samples of the 'evangelistic opportunity' argument discussed on pages 14-15 below. Unfortunately there was no speaker called to witness to the evangelistic effects of delaying baptism, or laying down conditions.

[2] For explanation and comment see footnote on page 23.

1. THE LIMITS OF INFANT BAPTISM

The above-mentioned essay (on 'The Church and Baptism') in *Evangelical Essays on Church and Sacraments* sets out six cumulative arguments for infant baptism as a principle. These may be listed (without being argued afresh) as follows:

1. The argument from the covenant with Abraham and the rite of circumcision.

2. The argument from the application of baptism at the very beginning of the Christian life.

3. The argument from the baptism of households in the New Testament.

4. The argument from the membership of the church enjoyed by young children in the New Testament.

5. The argument from the impossibility of bringing up children in Christian homes in any way other than as Christians.

6. The conceding of the point that infant baptism should lead onto more or less immediate admission to communion[1].

These points are not to be expanded here, but the reader is referred to the symposium in which they are located. For the moment two more New Testament shreds of evidence are added, not because they are weighty, but because they combine with the other lines of argument which point to the propriety of infant baptism, and because they coincide with these other lines of argument in their implications about the limits of infant baptism. They are as follows:

7. The argument from Acts 2.39. Here Peter says that the promise is 'to you and your children and to all who are far off'. At first sight this might well refer only to descendants, but it should be noted both that children might well be present at such a pilgrim feast, and also that the persons addressed by Peter included proselytes (verse 11)—a class of persons virtually never otherwise mentioned in the New Testament (cf. Mt. 23.15, Acts 6.5, 13.43). As proselytes they had themselves been baptised and circumcised with their children as their entry into judaism, and they are now invited to be baptised into the Christ who, they are told, is the heart of judaism. They are told the promise is to their children, the children are perhaps present with them, and they themselves are to be baptised. The probabilities suggest that such children would accompany them into the waters of baptism. But anyone disposed to resist the conclusion is of course free to do so. The conclusion is a very precarious one unless taken in conjunction with the other lines of argument above.

[1] There is of course no reliance placed upon Mark 10.13-16, etc. for this purpose.

8. The argument from 1 Cor. 7.14. The argument here takes as an agreed principle the 'holiness' of the child of one believing parent. It is of little weight towards establishing the propriety of infant baptism because parity of argument in the same passage would establish the 'holiness' of the unbelieving partner, whom few would want to admit to baptism. The passage remains a puzzle so far as any reference to qualifications for baptism is concerned. It is not used here to establish any cumulative force for the practice of infant baptism. It is only used to warrant a further inference *if* it does help qualify infants for baptism. The *'if'* remains.

If infant baptism itself is to be weighed in the balance then further arguments still must be deployed—for instance, arguments about the significance of New Testament silence, arguments about the salvation of infants who die, arguments from post-apostolic practice etc. To the writer these all add their weight to the conclusion. But they cannot be deployed properly without much space, and in this booklet the space is lacking, and the propriety of infant baptism as a principle is not the true theme. Hopes of writing the large tome have been frustrated over the years by other business, and hence the essay in the symposium mentioned, along with this brief discussion, are offered in the hope that something is better than nothing. But to do a proper apologia would take a large volume, and there is no real substitute.

Here then, we argue *from* infant baptism, not *to* it. And the major line of argument from it emerges at sight from the eight categories of evidence adduced above. It is simply that infant baptism is for those whose parents are themselves practising Christians. The arguments above each yield their own contribution to this conclusion, and it will be useful to go over them.

1. The circumcising of Ishmael, then of Isaac, and of Esau and Jacob was dependent in each case upon the father's being the man of God to whom and through whom the promises of God were made and implemented. Any parallels with baptism must start from the status of the parents before God before proceeding to infer the propriety of the baptism of their children.

2. The argument from the beginning of the Christian life is only relevant to infants where those infants are born (or adopted) into the context of a Christian home and family.

3. The baptism of households starts from certain facts about the parents or head of the household (i.e. that they are themselves converted) and proceeds from there to the baptism of the members of the household.

4. The children who were members of the church in New Testament days were not absolutely provably from Christian homes (Eph. 6. 1-3, Col. 3.20), though they were baptised (Eph. 4.5, Col. 2.12). But a fair reading at least suggests that the homes were Christian.

5. The argument about how Christian parents bring up their children is by definition an argument from the status of the parents.

6. Admission to communion for an infant or very young child can only be done by extending the parents' status of communicants to the child.

7. The argument from Acts. 2.39 assumes that the parents were being converted before any question as to what they did with their children can be allowed to arise.

8. The uncertain argument from 1 Cor. 7.14 also involves the foundation principle that the 'holiness' of children only arises from the believing status of (at least) one parent.

The purpose of re-listing these cumulative points now stands out very clearly. There is no warrant to baptise any infants but those of whom the parents (or one parent) are members of the church, practising, believing worshipping. Beyond that, no case for infant baptism can be made. The sacrament if administered in other cases is not invalid, but it is grossly misused and profaned.

At the same time the principles above set before the church the need to distinguish believers from unbelievers when application is made for baptism. This is the nettle the Church of England finds it so hard to grasp. Yet, without some grasping, indiscriminate baptism results. And therein lies a host of evils.

2. THE CASE FOR INDISCRIMINATE INFANT BAPTISM

At the Reformation the Anglican bishops were found ranged firmly against the Anabaptists. Their defence of infant baptism (e.g. in Article XXVII) may not have been very profound, but they themselves had no doubts on the subject. Their presupposition was of course that England was a Christian country. Settled 'Christendom' was the milieu for their liturgical and disciplinary rulings, and this led them to retain the medieval style of rubrics about the necessity of infant baptism. Thus the 1552 service of 'Private Baptism' begins with the instruction *'The Pastours and Curates shall oft admonishe the people that they deferre not the Baptisme of Infantes anye longer than the Sondaye, or other holye daye next after the chyld bee borne'*. The 1662 rubric is similar. The same approach is found in the 1604 Canons, nos 68 and 69 of which in effect warn the clergy not to leave any child unbaptised in the parish. The Reformers did not discuss the fate of unbaptised children who died (though the Ten Articles of 1536 had said such children were lost), but they were as determined as their predecessors that the event should not occur.

All this, whilst never well argued, was perfectly understandable on the basis of a 'christendom' concept of the nation. However, we have now inherited a situation where, although some Christian folklore remains at large in the national consciousness, yet the country shows no sign whatsoever of being roughly coextensive with the Christian Church (let alone the Church of England). The worshipping community is a small fraction of the total population, and in some areas the Church as a community has almost disappeared. The beginnings of this lie with the Industrial Revolution and even earlier. The latter stages have been accelerated by the rate of change in society, by urbanisation, and by large-scale immigration. England is now religiously pluriform, with the vast bulk of the people in some form of practical atheism.

Yet the Reformation practice of invariable infant baptism has continued, even when its *raison d'etre* has disappeared. There has been no point at which the Church of England could say with one voice 'We are now not the nation of England at prayer, but are less in numbers than the nation, and deeper in commitment than the nation'. There have been landmarks along the road—toleration of non-conformists in the seventeenth century, Catholic Emancipation in the nineteenth, the voluntary association implied in electoral rolls in the twentieth. But at many points the national role of the Church of England still exists on paper, and the will to tear up the paper has not emerged. Hence Englishmen may still feel that they have a right to baptism for their children (as well as to marriage and burial services when required) through the sheer weight of tradition and (if necessary) the bits of paper. The Church of England itself often uses Institution services which contain the following:

> *The Bishop:* It is the duty of the Minister frequently to admonish the people that they defer not the Baptism of their children; to seek out and bring any unbaptised persons in the parish to the Holy Sacrament of Baptism; and to catechize . . .

Services like this (the one from which this extract was taken was in use recently in London diocese, but it is fairly standard in the country) have usually been compiled in the last hundred years, and have thus deliberately built into the twentieth century the outlook appropriate to the 'christendom' situation of the sixteenth. When parents are not worshippers or otherwise noticeably Christian, then this 'duty of the Minister' runs clean contrary to any biblical principles which can be invoked. Fortunately, some tiny signs are now emerging that dioceses are unhappy with this sort of Institution service.

For it is only in the last twenty-five years that anyone within the Church of England (with two notable exceptions) has really expressed any hesitations about the indiscriminate practice of infant baptism. It was simply taken for granted as the Anglican way of doing things ,and justified in contradistinction to the Baptists as exemplifying the primacy of God's grace over man's response, and the free initiative of God towards men without discrimination. However, the two exceptions should be noted, both because of the stature of the men concerned, and also because of the relatively long time ago that they raised their protests.

Hensley Henson (later Bishop, first of Hereford, then of Durham), whilst still Vicar of Barking spoke as follows in a University sermon at Oxford on 14th June, 1896:

> 'The practice which works out to this miserable confusion, the modern practice of unconditioned, indiscriminate baptizing is indecent in itself, discreditable to the Church, and highly injurious to religion. . . . Certainly the scandalous laxity which presides over the admission of new members into the Divine Society augurs ill for the future discipline of those members. . . . It is not charity to indulge in the solemn mockery of their use in cases where the assumption of Christianity cannot be reasonably made; it is a grievous and baleful imposture. . . . Is it indeed to Christ that we bring these children, whom we so baptize that they never know they are Christ's? . . . I submit that our present laxity rather hinders than facilitates access to Christ'[1].

---

[1] Quoted in C. E. Pocknee *Infant Baptism Yesterday and To-day* (Mowbray 1966) pages 1-2.

The equally famous Roland Allen, who said of his books on missionary menthods that he did not expect them to come into their own until 50 years after they were written, resigned his incumbency of Chalfont St. Peter in 1907 over this issue of indiscriminate baptism. This action, like his books, was difficult to understand at the time. It is only too meaningful to-day.

These exceptions apart, indiscriminate baptism went unchallenged till after the Second War, and showed little sign of yielding to argument until the last decade. Even now, the majority of parishes in England are probably still virtually indiscriminate in their administration of infant baptism, and as recently as 1972, a learned incumbent, R. R. Osborn, could write a sustained plea for 'General Baptism' (*Forbid Them Not,* SPCK 1972).

What then can be said in favour of this inherited practice over against the limits of infant baptism deducible from Scripture? We marshall several arguments and examine them.

1. *'The law gives every Englishman the right to have his child baptised'.* The 'law' quoted here is in fact Canon 68 of 1604. The argument is weak at three points. Firstly, the Canons of 1604 were never part of Statute law, so that their enforceability as the law of the land is doubtful. Secondly, these Canons have in fact been superseded by the revised code of Canons of 1964 and 1969, and the new Canon B 22[1] allows discretion, at least to the Bishop, to refuse baptism for good reasons. It establishes no right in law. Thirdly, the law has never been tried in the sense of anyone asking for a court injunction requiring a minister to baptise his child. Failing such an action, it must remain very doubtful whether any or all Englishmen indiscriminately could have ever obtained such an injunction under the old Canons, and it is certain now that the Bishop's ruling is final. Thus the stated legal 'right' is probably non-existent.

   But in any case, resort to law by the minister is the way of the coward. If the action of a minister depends solely upon his insistence that his arm is twisted by the law, so that his conscience and theology are strictly irrelevant, then the minister concerned is obviously funking a facing of the issue on its merits. Not thus will the truth be found.

2. *'Infant baptism attests the primacy of the grace of God, and to deny the baptism is to deny the grace of God in such a case'.* We doubt whether in fact the statement 'Infant baptism attests the primacy of the grace of God' *tout simple* will suffice as a comprehensive theological assertion. Baptism, for instance, sets the boundaries of the visible church. Is it meaningful or sensible to throw them as wide as possible? Infant baptism, from Scripture, also attests the organic oneness of the Christian parents with their children. What does it attest when the parents are not

---

1 See the text set out in the Appendix on page 24.

detectably Christian? Infant baptism also involves the obligation to 'walk in newness of life'[1]. What meaning has this when nothing in the child's home context suggests that he will ever be aware of such obligation, let alone discharge it? Infant baptism attests many things, and its witness to most of them is blurred when it is administered indiscriminately.

Does it then really attest 'the primacy of the grace of God'? Of course God's grace is primacy. Of course any adult or infant who belongs to Christ does so because God by his providence and his Spirit sought and found the person with pre-venient grace. But no-one would dream of baptising an unbelieving adult to attest 'the primacy of God's grace'. Baptism is indeed a means and a declaration of grace, but it is only given to an adult when he shows some signs of believing, and of being drawn by God's love. And if adult baptism is not knowingly administered before men show signs of God's grace at work, then it is a poor argument to use to justify indiscriminate infant baptism. No doubt in a sense any rightly applied infant baptism does, as a side-effect of its application, 'attest the primacy of God's grace', but an incidental consequence of the right use of an ordinance cannot be turned into a justification of the wrong use of it. With adults and infants alike, we look for some rule-of-thumb warrant for baptising particular candidates. If the warrant exists then no doubt we are administering baptism in the wake of the signs of God's grace and favour, but as that is inevitable with adults on all showings, it ought not to be a problem in the case of infants. The warrant for baptising adults should be a professed desire to belong to Christ and to join his people, and the equivalent warrant for infants should be the existing status in Christ and his Church of the parents. In each case the warrant attests that God is at work towards the candidate, and the baptism attests that the Church has recognised this. Beyond this, it is hard to know what sort of grace indiscriminate baptism attests. Presumably, to use Bonhoeffer's phrase, only a very cheap grace.

1 To this it might be objected that the obligation to walk in newness of life (Romans 6.3-4) only arises from adult baptism. This is totally unconvincing. If there is a case for infant baptism at all (and there is) then the case is that the one and only baptism which is described in scripture is, in certain given circumstances, applicable to infants. Theologically it must be the same initiation which is happening, and in' principle any statements in Scripture about the meaning of baptism must be applicable to the infant case. If not, there is no case for infant baptism left in Scripture. If so, then baptism places the infant under the same Lordship of Christ which his parents acknowledge, and lays upon him the same obligation to walk in newness of life as the obligation others assume baptism at riper years. (This in turn requires that the promises and declarations in infant baptisms should belong to the *candidate*, though made by proxy, and should not in essence be the promises of someone else. There may be pastoral and disciplinary need for parents to make undertakings about how they will bring children up, but these undertakings are *not* the baptismal 'vows', and these latter must belong at least primarily to the candidate and to no-one else).

3. *'But is not an unbaptised child in danger if he dies?'* There are no cast-iron answers to this, but not because there is any reason to distinguish in terms of ultimate salvation between the unbaptised child who dies and the baptised one who dies. The problem is that Scripture gives us virtually no light on infant salvation in any case. When C. S. Lewis argues that the man who is glorified is the distillation of all in grace that that man had been through his life (and not just the perhaps senile person who was visible in his old age), then we have to ask what sort of person is an infant who has been glorified. Having asked it, we cannot answer it. We do not know what it means for an infant to be saved or lost. The nearest answer we can get will relate it to its parents. But then we are back at the point where baptism will do no personal good to a child of a non-Christian home, but may in fact allow the parents off the hook of responsibility for their baby's spiritual welfare. Certainly Christian parents should want to mark a child of theirs who is in danger of death as being one with them in the love of God, and as a Christian from earliest days, even if he dies. Baptism expresses all this admirably, and Christian parents should have their children, well or ill, baptised. (This is not to say that ministers should get involved in theological argument with parents who fear lest their child will die any minute, but it sets up principles to be followed whilst the child is healthy. Parents who are not themselves Christians can be told that baptism in such a context will not affect the child in respect of his ultimate salvation)

4. *'Administering infant baptism is part of our evangelistic contact and opportunity with unbelieving persons'.* This is a nakedly pragmatic justification. It disregards all questions about the meaning and relevance of baptism in particular contexts, and asks only whether a pastoral or evangelistic opportunity is created by accepting the child for baptism. If it consistently refuses to face the question as to whether on other grounds it is right or not to baptise the child, then the reason given is open to the charge of doing evil that good may come.

That of itself would be bad enough. But in addition it falls down when assessed by its own criterion. Generations of infants have been baptised by generations of clergy. Where are the fruits of the evangelistic contacts with the parents? Whilst no parish would lightly wish to set up a sense of rejection in those who had applied for their children to be baptised, yet equally it must be asked whether the sense of being accepted has brought such persons nearer to the kingdom. There is virtually no evidence to hand that any parish has flourished in its evangelism by a blithe acceptance of children for baptism.

Indeed the reverse may be the case. Michael Botting can write 'I have discovered from personal experience that there are real gains from a strict baptismal policy'[1]. It is not our task here to argue

---

[1] *Reaching the Families* (C.P.A.S. 1969) page 81, cf. page 21 below.

from results, because it is the cause of theology and truth which is at stake. But the results do not go all one way. If the gospel sacrament of baptism is being maladministered, can we look for the gospel to be really flourishing as a result?

5. *'The Church must never refuse Baptism if sincerely desired for their child by its parents or guardians'*. This principle is quoted from the report of the Ely Commission *(Christian Initiation: Birth and Growth in the Christian Society,* page 35). Whilst its basic intention is to safeguard baptism against too indiscriminate a use, this statement of principle in fact allows a wholesale return to the practice of almost universal baptism. A footnote to this statement about 'sincere desire' says that it means 'a genuine longing that the child may enter into the Christian community' and may properly be tested by the parents' readiness to receive preparation. Quite apart from the vagueness of the criterion about preparation, this completely sidesteps the well-attested phenomenon that parents who want their child baptised will always insist they are 'sincere' and 'genuine', and will not usually mind going along with a preparation class or visit. The Ely Commission is near to the right question, but it seems hopelessly far from the right answer, as its criterion of sincerity is so loose.

Most of these sorts of arguments are rationalisations adopted to justify failure to grasp the nettle. Against these points we may note five factors in the larger context. They should be set against the arguments above and should give their proponents pause.

1. Indiscriminate infant baptism divorces baptism from the gospel. In the Scriptures baptism clinches the gospel offer, and belongs with it (cf. Acts 2.38). If there are children to be baptised it is not because they are merely entitled to *hear* the gospel (which all men are), but because they are already involved in *accepting* the gospel, at least so far as the human eye can see. Once the administration of baptism runs beyond the effective administration of the gospel both the ordinance and the message are seriously undermined. Indeed baptism becomes either a charm or else strictly incredible.

2. Indiscriminate infant baptism removes all credible boundaries from the visible church. This is obvious, and it means in turn that it is hard for the church to be the church.

3. Indiscriminate infant baptism so devalues the sacrament as to make it meaningless for adults. The 'oneness' of the sacrament is impossible to demonstrate, and to make the sacrament meaningful for an adult it has to be split off from infant baptism. This is a way of disintegration.

4. Indiscriminate infant baptism loses some of the Church of England's best Church members. They go and become Baptists. This is not because they have necessarily rejected the principle of infant baptism when it is properly administered. It is because *they have*

never seen it properly administered, and thus do not know what the basic principles are. The abuse of infant baptism is so widespread that it has become almost an esoteric theological task to set up a rationale for its proper use. Certainly most worshippers would not be able to discern the proper use of infant baptism from its practice in their own congregation. Hardly surprising then that many reject infant baptism out of hand and become Baptists. Any weighing up of the question of 'results' must take into account the fine Christian people who are currently lost to their local parish Church and flee instead (often to a considerable distance) to find a Baptist congregation where baptism apparently means something.

5. Indiscriminate infant baptism penalises the recipients of the rite. This is not so much because it is likely to deceive them into thinking they are all right with God simply because they are baptised. This may have been the problem in the past, but in times when growing youngsters have hardly heard of God, care nothing about being right with him, and are almost certainly ignorant as to whether they are baptised or not, this is not the problem of to-day or to-morrow. The point of penalising is if and when youngsters from unbelieving homes ever become Christians. If so, it will be by genuine conversion, not by Christian upbringing. And if this is so, then the conversion should be marked, established and sealed by baptism. A new convert is most likely to need this point of no return provided in baptism, and has difficulty in understanding the value of a far past infant baptism which never brought him into actual relationship with God or his people.

To summarise we may note that the admission of the unqualified to baptism is a perversion of Christian principles. It is a form of unreflecting situation ethics. The 'situationist' is always concerned to help the person he is counselling in that person's own situation. The principles along which advice is given are principles derived from the man's situation, and designed to help him in it. And this sounds like the way of love.

However, the difficulty with 'situations' is that they do not stop at the four walls of the counselling room. The situation concerned is not only, say, one unhappy marriage—it is also the whole of the Church's stance over marriage, it is also some hundreds of thousands of other homes, and it is also thousands more people preparing for marriage. All these may be affected by decisions over particular cases. And so it is with baptism. Although a minister may have much sympathy for parents who want their child baptised yet have no visible Christian qualifications for this, he is in fact taking decisions in a far larger situation than just the dealing with one couple.

When we have said this, it is not enough. For although the 'situation' itself, when seen aright, requires a very discriminate practice of infant baptism, yet in truth situations should not decide theological questions at all. If the New Testament sets up principles, then it is our task to apply them. And what can then justify the indiscriminate practice?

3. GOALS

In chapter 1 above the conclusion of the biblical case was summarised thus: 'There is no warrant to baptise any infants but those of whom the parents (or one parent) are members of the church, practising, believing, worshipping. Beyond that, no case for infant baptism can be made'. This conclusion sets up for us the requisite goals for which to aim.

Believers are to be distinguished from unbelievers amongst the parents. How is this to be done? The simple and obvious answer (for the sake of clarifying goals) is that in formal and outward terms a Christian is a communicant, and *vice versa*. The parents are to be living members of the church by communion if the children are to be newborn members of the church by baptism. There is no other way. Not only in the New Testament is the sacrament of communion the characteristic activity of the people of God, but also the times of to-day demand that the church be measured by some formal means. Communion requires persons to 'stand up and be counted'. It is a semi-public activity with specific participation. Listening to sermons does not necessarily imply commitment or even agreement. But participation in communion implies both. If baptism sets formal boundaries to the visible church, then communion sustains and corrects them week by week. Where there is a faithful company at the Lord's Table, there is the church. And where there is the church, then children of its members may be and should be admitted to baptism.

This means that communion must take its rightful place in the life of the church. If it is an occasional activity only, then it never becomes part of the rhythm of life for believers. Where it is a 'staying-behind' activity, then this very fact indicates that it is simply for the extra-devout, or those with time to spare. Where it is a 'main service' once a month, it may still have the nature of an 'offer' for those who happen to care for that sort of thing. The sanction of the Lord's command 'do this' is never applied.

Therefore it is a presupposition to getting infant baptism right that we also get communion right. Unless it is the central service of the Sunday, then it never becomes the basic rhythm of corporate Christian life. And in turn it never sets up the requisite test of whether parents are 'members of the church, practising, believing, worshipping'.[1]

Goals are easier to state than achieve. And the goal in relation to infant baptism is as yet only half-stated. For ultimately a baptismal policy must not be that of any one parish or congregation, it must be that of the whole church of God. There must be a solidarity of practice across the whole face of the church. Parents must know that wherever they go, the same

---

1 Infant and child communion is not the theme of this booklet, but it will be obvious how it arises naturally from the considerations above. On the one hand, children being treated as Christian in baptism will then continue to be treated as Christian in communion; on the other, their parents' regular participation in communion will naturally involve their children from the start. Granted the context of communicating parents there is no problem here at all. Thus we happily reject the supposed objection to infant baptism (see page 7 above) that those who urge infant baptism cannot really believe in it because they refuse its natural corollary, infant and child communion.

demands of practising membership will be made of them. And if disunity persists, then the goal must include all those who practise infant baptism.[1]

How then can this sort of goal be achieved? Not by wholesale change overnight. That is not the plea of this booklet. Goals are set out in order that thinking may be kept clear, and proper directions for change established. But this is far from dictating a timetable for changes, or holding a gun to people's heads. Change must often come in an evolutionary way in the church, and we can well be content with the less-than-perfect at any particular time, so long as we are sure that the right directions for reform are being pursued, and the matter is in trend. (This is comparable to the quest for doctrinal purity in the church, or sinless perfection in the individual—we know the nature of the goal in principle, but we live in tension, making progress and keeping alive a strong eschatological hope of achieving the goal. But it *is* eschatological, and the hope re baptismal policy may be too). In particular, reforms in the church have to have not only the right content, but also the right procedures. To take an absurd example:— although the Reformation was implemented in England by the will of Monarchs and Councils and enforced by Acts of Parliament, and many have been very grateful for the results of their labours, nobody could now want Parliament to force upon the Church of England any sort of reforms at all, even if they were reforms he personally greatly desired. In the baptismal field the danger is that the parson, suffering from a conscience about whom he is baptising, may want to take unilateral action. The right decisions taken by the wrong persons can be wrong decisions. It is no part of the thesis of this booklet that goals must be achieved by any means so long as they are achieved to-morrow!

Yet there is also the opposite danger—that no-one will feel competent to make any changes at all There are signs at the time of writing that in the Church of England this is beginning to develop in a tension between the centre and the parishes. There has been no central policy for the Church of England[2] and the main assumption has been that policy would grow up from the parishes, first to the deaneries, then to the dioceses (the level it has already reached in Chelmsford and London), and perhaps finally to the General Synod. On the other hand, one now finds more and more clergy asking for a national policy to be imposed, in order that they may have some authority in tackling the question on the local front. Thus the parishes and the centre alike may be waiting for the others to act. It is pioneering which is difficult, and falling into line is easier.

The case is thus set out not only that goals must be approached by the right means, but also that the right procedures must be found for implementing the means. That is the theme of the next chapter.

---

[1] It may be harder to visualise Methodists setting up a test of being a communicant than even evangelical Anglicans. If so, then the goal is further off, but it is still the goal.

[2] The Canons quoted cited earlier and set out on page 24 can hardly be called a policy. The prefatory rubrics to *Series 2* infant baptism service certainly provide an *instrument* for a policy. But they hardly of themselves constitute such a policy. The Ely and Doctrine Commissions again have skirted round the questions of a policy and have simply provided material which would be useful in the operation of a policy. They cannot be said of themselves to have laid out any proposals for a central policy. Overall the emphasis is upon helping parishes to have local parish policies.

4. MEANS AND PROCEDURES

How do we get from where we are to where we ought to be? This is the perennial problem of would-be reformers. It is the task of this chapter to suggest paths or routes to the goals set up, though such suggestions are made in full awareness both of the great variety of parishes to be found in the Church of England, and also that other means may also be available and those set out are by no means an exclusive list.

The problem is first of all the parson's, as the situation stands. Parents approach him for their child's baptism. He does the baptism. He is the point of contact. And he bears the responsibility both for whether or not to do the baptism, and also for making the best use of the contact.

But it is not only that. Because a very heavy preponderance of baptisms is still performed at 4 p.m. or thereabouts, in what is really not a congregational service at all, the parson is often the only person who knows the size and shape of the problem. Whilst 4 p.m. baptisms continue the vast bulk of church people will only be present at the less frequent genuinely public baptisms at main services. As these are likely to be for the children of *bona fide* church members the baptisms may seem entirely appropriate, and there is no problem. Even churchwardens and readers may be ignorant of the size of the problem which exists behind the scenes and the resultant strain on the incumbent's conscience.

So what can the parson do on his own initiative? Obviously he should observe his parochial boundaries and not baptise infants from outside his parish[1]. But it is almost equally obvious that he should perform infant baptisms in public, at full main services. This of itself may make a small percentage of parents withdraw. But it may still leave relatively large numbers seeking baptism. The proposal here is that however daunting the numbers, the incumbent should still persist with this policy. It may mean that very large numbers are presented for baptism on each baptismal occasion. But it need not mean that the occasions themselves come very frequently. They might be one month at a main morning service, and the next at an evening one. Or, where there are three main services (including, e.g. in the morning both a family service and a Morning Prayer, or a Parish Communion and a Morning Prayer), then each might have the baptisms

---

1 The proper exception to this is the case of parents on the electoral roll of the parish. As they must worship regularly in the parish for six months, they become real members of the church there. As electoral rolls are being made up from scratch again in 1972, there is no danger of those who got on an electoral roll years ago, in order to get married in a particular Parish Church, returning now and claiming the right to have their offspring, born and belonging 100 miles away, baptised there. But electoral rolls must be kept up to date or this problem will recur. When newly-weds settle down and begin to raise a family they either belong to their local church or they do not. In the former case they should have their baptisms locally, in the latter they are not entitled to seek them elsewhere. See Canon B 22 paragraph 5, quoted on page 24.

once a quarter. There can well be provision for making the administration quick and smooth, but the important thing is that the parents have to behave like worshippers in the congregation (which is the assumption in accepting them as qualifying their child for baptism), the baptism more vividly incorporates the child into the ongoing life of the church, and the congregation starts to understand the size of the problem.

Obviously a congregation must be prepared for such a change. But once they are prepared and are accepting it, then the problem can be shared with the Parochial Church Council, or the Annual Church Meeting. Up till then the minister has wrestled with his conscience on his own—now it is the responsibility of the local church. If the local church simply accepts that all and sundry can bring their children to these public baptisms then little further progress can be made. But the chances are that a church with any spiritual life will discern the discrepancy between the frequent lack of Christian religion on the one hand, and the presence of the desire for baptism on the other. This places a dual responsibility upon the local church—responsibility for ministering the gospel to those who are seeking baptism, and responsibility for safeguarding baptism from abuse. And it is well that the responsibility should lie upon the local church rather than the minister—it is right theologically (for the body must act as a totality and in harmony), and it is right pragmatically because otherwise a change of minister may cause an about-turn in policy. Policy must be that of the church, and for these purposes of the *local* church. This in turn means that the P.C.C. must bear the main weight.

What then can the local church do? Despite traditions and Canons they would be unwise to rely upon tightening up standards for godparents. Godparents are without the requisite influence upon growing children. If local Christians stand as sponsors at infant baptisms, they may well quickly find themselves 100 miles from the children, as population shifts so quickly. Only the frailest of contacts is established by this sponsorship, and it can sustain no weight.[1]

A P.C.C. may also establish a pattern of visitation and preparation which enables parents to understand the nature of baptism, and leaves them to decide whether they want it for their child or not. It would be appropriate if much of the visitation and preparation could be done by lay persons, though there is little sign of this happening so far. But experience shows that those who desire baptism (who can say whether they desire it sincerely?) are ready to say almost anything in order to obtain it. Indeed

---

[1] This is putting the matter pragmatically. But in dogmatic terms also, we should note that the sponsors have no scriptural place and should not be thought to be undertaking anything about the child's upbringing. They *may* be witnesses to the parents' faith (which can hardly be the role envisaged where non-worshippers are presenting their children for baptism), and they are able to take a proxy role for the children at the baptism itself. They may pray for a child (and should). They may give Christmas presents (and perhaps should). They may be able to adopt in the event of the parents' death (and this is a real link). But they are at the most first reserves—never substitutes.

there are complaints sometimes heard that *Series* 2 infant baptism service has so clearly spelled out the requirements that it deliberately encourages people in hypocrisy! Obviously the service cannot be whittled down to involve little or no commitment in order that it may meet an eccentric pastoral situation, but the very complaint shows how thousands will blandly assent to *anything* in order to secure the baptism. No doubt more and more are not now bringing children for baptism at all. No doubt some may be daunted from baptism when its terms are clearly expressed. But a great number will still assent to the terms outwardly in order to have their offspring baptised.

It is at this point that an alternative to baptism may be considered. Neither the Ely Commission nor the Doctrine Commission were prepared to use the word 'alternative', but this is what parishes may need. This is more or less how the Chelmsford provision operates. On this basis all parents are offered some ministration by the church, and whether or not the ministration should include the totality of the claims of baptism upon a child's life is for them to decide. Again, to have a team of lay people visit and explain may be extremely helpful.[1]

Yet all this still leaves decisions with the parents. Are there ways in which a P.C.C. can and should go further, and themselves insist that certain qualifications should be met before a child is eligible for baptism? In Michael Botting's London parish, St. Matthew's Fulham, he and his P.C.C., having tried preparation classes without affecting the apparent pressure for baptism from non-worshipping parents, made a clear rule: if parents were to take Christian obligations upon their children, they must first take them upon themselves. Thus at least one parent must be prepared for adult confirmation, and, as part of the preparation for adult confirmation, the family must take its place in the regular worship of the church, probably at the weekly family service[2]. Thus a pattern of instruction and worship was set up which directed parents towards professing their own faith at confirmation, and then being regular communicants. This in turn qualified their children for baptism. A steady trickle of adults was converted by this means, which suggests that it is not necessarily the being prepared to baptise which gives the evangelistic opportunity. The evidence suggests that it does not, but a baptismal policy does. The evangelism is more clearcut and the terms more fully understood in such a case.

1 The contents and use of such a service of 'Thanksgiving' are taken up in Booklet No. 5 in this series—*A Service of Thanksgiving and Blessing* by C. H. B. Byworth and J. A. Simpson (2nd edition, 1974).
2 See Botting *Reaching the Families* (C.P.A.S. 1969).

The policy at St. Matthew's Fullham is not necessarily imitable elsewhere. In suburbia a larger proportion of parents may already be confirmed, and would thus qualify their children without further ado. The Fulham policy was geared to a particular need, and it included the non-sacramental family service as the liturgical threshold to being communicant. Elsewhere the weekly communion may prove more and more to be a family communion, with the children participating in the reception of the elements[1]. In such a pattern of Sunday worship, unbelievers *may* come into the family communion with their children, or they *may* start at some evening service without them. But the assumption underlying such a Sunday pattern is that primary evangelism will not be conducted so much through services as in homes and other places where people may meet informally. If people wish to be enquirers then by all means they may go to a non-sacramental service (or to a sacramental service without receiving communion), but this will be by no means necessary. The point of full commitment can be reached with virtually no preceding attendance upon Sunday liturgical services because evangelism has been conducted outside the worship building. When it is reached, then adults who are already baptised will be simply admitted to communion—those who are not baptised will first be baptised and thus be admitted to communion. Both sets will take their children into baptism, as parents who are themselves already communicant will. But the uncommitted, that is to say the unbaptised and the non-communicating, will not. They will be directed first into some discussion of what it means to be baptised and communicant.

To move towards this point, which in parochial terms is almost exactly the attaining of the goal of the previous chapter, there must be complete oneness of mind on a P.C.C. If local residents can ask for baptism, and find senior members of the local church unable to defend or explain the church's policy, then the policy is doomed. To restrict baptism to the qualified is only possible where the church has a common mind, and is able to communicate it readily. If the policy is inconsistently applied, dependent upon interior judgments, or simply inexplicable, it will cause real offence and wreak damage in the life of the congregation itself. This is why a parish is urged to go as one, even if slowly, rather than have the incumbent, or conceivably some lay person, institute a policy of his own, which has not been talked through or agreed in the church itself.

There was, however, a further goal—the goal of agreement over a whole area, or indeed (strictly as a goal) over the whole face of the earth! This raises the question of procedures. Here the initiative lies with the local church (despite the above-mentioned desire of some clergy to be 'directed' from the centre). No parish can institute a baptismal policy effectively without raising it at the deanery. A deanery Synod in turn should refer the question (and perhaps some suggested answers) to every P.C.C. in the deanery. Nothing should go up to the diocese till there is agreement solidifying in the deanery. When there is, it should also be raised with the other denominations in the area which practice infant baptism, and their

---

[1] Though not, one would hope, necessarily having to sit through an adult sermon earlier in the service. Children should be given separate instruction during the 'Ministry of the Word' section of the communion service.

promise to restrict infant baptism to the offspring of their own members should be sought. And the matter can then go to the diocese. When a diocese has in turn had the matter tackled through all its deaneries, then it can go to General Synod. General Synod in turn should refer the matter to the dioceses at large before attempting to form a national policy. And policies may be very mild initially, and reach national level in that form. If so, they can become progressively more definite, so that a new wave of policy-making and implementation can be started at the parish and deanery level, while the first wave is still being handled at the centre.

And the upshot? Occasionally one hears a minister speak with relief of falling numbers of baptisms. His relief is of course relative. The kingdom of God is not brought in by reducing the numbers of baptisms any more than it is by keeping the finances of a church in good order. No-one pretends that either of these is direct evangelism (though there is good reason to suppose that the kingdom of God is *hindered* by indiscriminate infant baptism, just as it is by failures in accurate book-keeping). The point is that the reduction in baptisms not only relieves the sorely-tried consciences of the clergy—it also enables baptism to be baptism and the church to be the church. And that in turn is the key to evangelism and service, to building up the people of God in love and in truth, and in the last analysis to bringing glory to God himself.

EXTENDED FOOTNOTE BELONGING TO PAGE 6

1 The actual reason for the extension to Series 2 was that a Series 3 text had been prepared by the Liturgical Commission but delayed by the House of Bishops until the Initiation debates were completed. In one sense therefore it would be possible for the Commission to reword the baptismal interrogations. But the question is, How? In fact there seems a wide-spread *approval* of these forms, and it is arguable that although no-one in Synod put down an amendment to remove the words referring to the Liturgical Commission, yet equally no-one would have minded if they had not been there. The matter is doubly paradoxical as the dioceses have been invoked at the same time as the Commission (and might take a different view). The cynic would suggest that the only form of interrogation which would give direct expression to a 'baptism-on-request' policy would be one which started with the question:

> 'Are you prepared to say "yes" to any further questions I ask, irrespective of content?'

In fact, of course, it may be that the 'and able' means that the Commission has no need to change anything.

I hope to write a full discussion of principles of baptismal liturgies in a commentary on Series 3 baptism services when they are finally published.

APPENDIX—Some documentation

A. Canon B 22 Of the Baptism of Infants

1. Due Notice, normally of at least a week, shall be given before a child is brought to the church to be baptized.
2. If the minister shall refuse or unduly delay to baptize any such infant, the parents or guardians may apply to the bishop of the diocese, who shall, after consultation with the minister, give such directions as he thinks fit.
3. The minister shall instruct the parents or guardians of an infant to be admitted to Holy Baptism that the same responsibilities rest on them as are in the service of Holy Baptism required of the godparents.
4. No minister shall refuse or, save for the purpose of preparing or instructing the parents or guardians or godparents, delay to baptize any infant within his cure that is brought to the church to be baptized, provided that due notice has been given and the provisions relating to godparents in these Canons are observed.
5. A minister who intends to baptize any infant whose parents are residing outside the boundaries of his cure, unless the names of such persons or of one of them be on the church electoral roll of the same, shall not proceed to the baptism without having sought the good will of the minister of the parish in which such parents reside.

(Paragraphs 6-9 concern private baptisms)

B. The Keele Statement—Infant Baptism

71. We affirm our belief in the scriptural foundation of infant baptism, but declare that only the children of parents who profess to be Christians are fit subjects for this rite. Indiscriminate infant baptism, as commonly practised in England, is a scandal, and is incidentally productive of much of the current divisive reaction against the baptizing of infants. We call now for a theologically-inspired national practice of baptismal discipline.

    We must be welcoming to little children, as Jesus was. But we deny the propriety of baptizing the infants of parents who do not profess to be Christians themselves and who cannot promise to bring up their children as Christians. We approve the proposals regarding Christian parenthood and upbringing which are embodied in the Preface to the new Service of Infant Baptism.

    In view of the widespread misunderstanding caused by such expressions as 'this child is regenerate', we would welcome their revision, provided that the covenant basis which they express is not lost.[1]

Public Baptism

72. We urge that baptism should always be held at the public services of the Church, unless there are compelling reasons to the contrary.

C. Series 2—Infant Baptism Para. 38 *The Preface*

It is the practice of the Church of England to admit to Baptism those who are not old enough to profess the Christian faith. But this is done on the understanding that they will receive a Christian upbringing. This means that they will be taught the Christian religion and encouraged to practise it, until such time as they present themselves to the Bishop for Confirmation, and publicly profess the faith in which they have been baptized.

Before proceeding to baptize a child, the Priest shall ask the parents and sponsors whether he has been baptized before. He shall also ask them:

whether they are prepared to the best of their ability to give him a Christian upbringing within the family of Christ's Church; whether they will help him to be regular in public worship and in private prayer, not only by their teaching, but also by their example and their prayers; whether they will encourage him in due time to come to Confirmation and Communion.

---

1. This particular desire of the evangelicals at Keele must rank as a backward-looking one. The whole implication of a baptismal discipline, for which they had just called, is that the liturgical declarations (such as that cited) would become more and more meaningful and authentic. Conversely to remove all such categorical language from the baptismal service would be counter-productive in terms of the quest for a discipline. A baptismal service which affirmed no new birth for the candidates would (like the 'Thanksgiving' service) be appropriate to every baby in the land, and would consequently cease to prod the clergyman's conscience. The thrust of this booklet is to let baptism be baptism. And the language of baptism is crucial to that thrust.